love letters to myself

sahara i. mehdi

BookLeaf Publishing
India | USA | UK

Presentation by *BookLeaf Publishing*

Web: www.bookleafpub.com

E-mail: info@bookleafpub.com

ISBN: 9789357447034

First edition 2022

this book is dedicated to the people
who have inspired these poems.

although i've never been in a romantic
relationship, i've written a lot of poetry
about love.

here's to living and loving and
writing about it all.

preface

i have a fatal flaw
(a *hamartia*, if you will)
i care too much

and too deeply
my heart is not a gradient scale
it is an on and off switch

i do not smile, i grin
i do not giggle
i laugh with my head leaned back

i do not cry
i sob, i heave breaths
until there are none left

i do not love
i do not love
i do not love

i fall
i fall too deep
i feel too deep

- the tragic lover

there is a wolf in my brain
and she has sharp claws
that grab onto every part
of myself that i don't like

and eyes that catch every glance in my direction
and ears so big they hear every insult
and teeth so sharp they bite into
any shred of self-love i have

but worse than her bite
is her bark
because all i can hear is
her telling me that i'm not good enough

not pretty enough
not smart enough
not kind enough
that i'm a fake

that i'm a liar
that i'm being lied to
that *no one*
wants me around

she makes her way into the people i love
turns their words into insults
turns their praise
into backhanded compliments

i ask her why
they act like they love me
and she says "only to fool you better, dear"
"only to use you better, dear"

"only to cheat you
and pull you apart
and break you into bite-sized pieces
to eat you better, my dear"

there is a wolf in my brain
and late at night when her howls
are the only thing that fill my mind
it's hard to remember that she's not real

that she's a figment
of my imagination
she's nothing but a myth
a fairy tale

and it doesn't matter
she feels real
she felt real
she will continue to feel real

but i have to
convince myself
she isn't
because i don't want to be

trapped by her claws
scrutinized by her gaze
overheard by her ears
chewed up by her teeth

more than that
i have to convince myself she isn't real
because i don't want to be
    -    *the girl who cried wolf*

i don't write poems about
my crushes
about infatuation
or the tingling feeling
in your stomach
when you see *them*

i don't write poems about
"i love you"s
or shy glances across a classroom
or the one who you are
meant to be with
forever

i write poems about love lost
about heartbreak
about the sinking feeling
in my stomach
or my brain
i can't decide

i write to make you fall apart
i write to shatter you
into a million pieces
i write to heal
i write to put you
back together

it's not that i'm above love
or that i haven't loved
or that i won't ever be in love
it's that i have
a strong inkling
that i can't be loved

i have been cherished by my parents
and doted on by teachers
and thanked by friends
i have been texted and told
and whispered to
"i love you" many a time

but i can't be loved
i am sure of this fact
i am not
a horrible person
evil does not flow through my veins

only love,
for i have so much to give
and yet none to take
do not look at me with pity
say you love me when
you don't mean it

because i know,
i know i can't be loved
because i
have tried so hard
and have been met
with defeat

-     *on self-love*

i want a love where we drive up north
to look at the galaxy in open fields
under open skies with open hearts
and childlike wonder shining in our eyes

i want you to take my breath away, darling
bathe me in starlight, i want to feel weightless
like we are up on the moon, like we are floating
like gravity has disappeared

like i can't remember which way is up
take me far away, honey
i want to feel like we just
discovered a new planet

i want a love that makes us wonder why
everyone else is still on earth
while we are drifting into our own orbit
i want something grand

i want it to be unrequited or heartbreaking
i want it to ruin me
i want anything that can
eclipse this feeling of empty

i want to escape this black hole of loneliness
i want to remind my heart that it is just
a single speck in the grand universe
and that there is so much more to be seen

-    *i want an astronomical love*

i was within and without
within your gaze, but without your company
in your mind yet somehow out of reach

i have always been within and without
tell me how you have known me all this time
and still have questions to ask me

within and without,
your eyes catching mine across a room
your intent gaze pulling me towards you

i've acquainted myself with
how your eyes widen when you see me
i've become familiar with your surprise

i've been looking across the bay and wondering,
has that green light always been so bright?
have you been watching it as well?

within and without, a laugh in your direction
a smile that fills me up like flowers blooming
your voice softening, is it serendipity?

have you always been this kind?
has your heart always beat that loud?
how are you so new but so known?

loud laughter and missing curfew by a minute
how many times have i rolled my eyes at you?
how many ways can you call my name tonight?

i look at you and feel like i am young again
and yet the space between who we were then
and who we are tonight feels infinite

i keep wondering
how we should fit now
like friends? like more?

i am still within and without
so go ahead, darling
decide where you want me

- *across the bay*

i think of you
your arm falling around me so naturally
or the way you stand in front of me
close enough that i have nowhere else
to look but right at you

i think of us driving around through towns
as if we have somewhere to go (we don't)
i tell you to take me to new york city
and you say yes
and that is the reason

i'm addicted to you, love
and as the serpentine roads in front of us
twist and turn into possibility
i can't but help but think
you are so tempting

you always say yes
it is my favourite part of us
and it makes me wonder:
what else would you
possibly say yes to?

- *let's pretend we're in love*

you remind me
of a sunrise
colours blending together
to create a beautiful mess

blue for the calm quiet of early morning
pink for my blushing cheeks
yellow for your smile
and orange for your laugh

red for the way you've invaded my heart
interrupted my bloodstream
made my heartbeats sound like your name
until my veins are filled with you

i lose myself in your magic
every morning when i look outside the window
and see you staring back at me
beckoning me into the brand new day

you remind me
of a sunset
colours meshing together
for a grand finale

blue for the ocean,
whose tides will soon be pulled by the moon
the same way my heartstrings pull for you,
pink for the sweetness of the sun

yellow that reminisces
over our happiest moments
orange that burns
like the embers of a fire

red like the roses
that i picked for you
the flowers will fade
and rot and die away

but the scent will linger
in the air just
a second too long
reminding you of my love

i fall for your grandeur once again
every evening as i'm walking home
watching you perform your last goodbye
to sing me to sleep

    -    *you are the sun*

you were never part of the plan
just a pit stop along the way
that's what i told myself
when the compass in my heart
led me to you

you were never part of the plan
but i'm not too great at directions
we're on a highway to disaster
and i'm bracing myself
for the inevitable crash

you were never part of the plan
but all roads take me to you
so i say it's about the journey
and we spend another night
driving around with nowhere to go

you were never part of the plan
but i should've known that
i always get lost
when my brain tries to map out
the route for my heart

  - *road map*

i take note of information about you
like i'm cramming for an exam
the way your eyes look in the sunlight
how you like your tea
play the way you say my name
over and over again until it sticks

i tell myself i'm remembering it
for some future
we'll never have together
i guess i'm saving it
for the day
i have to lose you

-     *studying you*

the line beeps twice to tell me you've hung up
and i already miss the sound of your voice
or the silence on the other end
as i tell you what i think of love at first sight

i say i don't believe in it
because i don't
i believe i fell in the late night conversations
fell in the hours where it became too dark to lie

fell into you
and so love at first sight never made sense to me
because i loved you after hours and hours
of hearing you on the other end

-    *(647) 735-5359*

for years, i've had a file of unfinished poems
so, you see, all of these phrases
had already been written down
scattered throughout my phone
and my brain and my journals

but, i couldn't fit the puzzle pieces together
i could never make them click
until i met you, and all the parts
of this love story i wrote for myself
finally made sense

when i think about you
my brain only speaks to me in poetry
i want to write sestinas
about the way your eyes change colours
haikus using the language we've created

sonnets on the way you smile at me knowingly
or the way you say "we" like a team
i know you're not a poet
but every single part of you
seems to be made up of poetry

-    *the poet's lover*

we are complete opposites, you see
i am in a rush, you say:
"let's take the long way"
i speed walk and you are lax,
stopping to speak to
strangers on the street

and every time i think you're gone
you catch up to me, swinging around
a dirty grey lamppost
like a scene from a musical
and i think this must be a dream
but it feels a lot like a nightmare

you are charming with smiling eyes
you tell me about how your parents fell in love
and i am scared of
what this could mean
i am afraid of what
we could become

i wonder who this girl
you call your friend really is
because i don't know her
she is me but with walls up
she won't let you know
anything about her

she laughs airily as if you haven't
understood a part of her
that she's tried to hide away
she stiffens when you come near
as if she doesn't want to be
melted by your touch

she looks away as if she couldn't
look into your eyes for eternity
you hold her close and tell her
everything is going to be alright
and she thinks to herself,
"how did someone manage to move
the once great and unshakable me"

-    *the treacherous heart*

you ask if i'm tired
and i say yes
even though i know it's not true

but if tired is leaning my head on your shoulder
and lazy afternoons in the city
then yes, my love, i'm exhausted

and i guess my bed is comfortable
but it's not your head heavy against mine
and it doesn't sound like your even breathing

it doesn't feel like sunshine on my face
it's not warmth and love
it doesn't feel like home

i find myself yawning as we drive home
and you roll your eyes because it's only 5 pm
but i say i'm tired

so i fall asleep in your arms
and hope this day and you
are a dream that will last forever

-    *i could never be tired of you*

there you are, pulling me closer
saving me a seat
introducing me to people as your
best friend since we were two

the chaos surrounds us
the noise is too loud
and the world is on fire
but we are not

and there you are, laughing at every joke
smiling with your eyes all crinkled
making moments for me even when
time feels like it is running out

and i feel alone too often
you feel misunderstood
but when we are together
we are not

and there you are, the one thing
i will never be able to lose
and there you are,
my home with a beating heart

we rush into another night, another adventure
breathless and laughing and scared
and everything else in this life is temporary
but we are not, my love, we are not

   -   *home with a beating heart*

when i say "come home"
what i mean is i want you close
i want you exactly 2.2 kilometres away
so that when we fall asleep
it is under the same sky
of half-hidden stars

when i say "come home"
i mean to say: i want you
the same way a moth
gravitates towards light
i mean to say: i need you
like gravity to keep me grounded

when i say "come home"
i mean: i want to relive last summer
i mean: i want the person who left me behind
i mean: i want us, the way we were
before everything changed
and our worlds split apart

-    *the end of september*

it's raining here
a huge thunderstorm like the night you left
and i think of you

but where you live now
the sky is clear
and you're not thinking of me

maybe that's what describes us most right now
two hearts, far away from each other
one more alone than the other

-    *two thousand kilometres too far*

you call me when you should
be on the phone with her
text me when she should
be the one you want to talk to
sit beside me when you should
be right next to her

i hope she appreciates
the suit i picked out
hope she falls for
the messages i write
hope she swoons over
the words i tell you to say

i hope she loves
the things i make you do
hope she treasures
the facade i've helped you falsify
hope she thinks
you are her forever

i hope she never realizes
she is the free trial
you didn't want to spend on
i hope she never realizes
i'm the one asking you
to do these things for her

i hope she lives in

her blissful ignorance
until the day you realize
you should be
doing all of this
for me

    -   *free trial*

i think it's funny
that you say
she could be
your happiness

i tell you that
you're looking for
knock-off versions
of forever

when i want to say
you're really looking
for knock-off versions
of me

-       *you can't get a second free trial*

and i wonder if you still keep
old love island episodes
recorded on your DVR for me
with the hope that one day i'll come over and
we'll spend the day together watching bad TV

the thought is a reminder of what we were —
grand promises, waiting to be broken,
the kind i believed in,
the ones you never intended to keep —
we were what would happen if friends
could be just as star-crossed as lovers

i wonder if you knew what i meant
when i sent that final text
i told you that i needed time and space
and maybe a break
(i don't remember the exact wording
but it was cliché)
did you think i was being sincere
when i said it was me and not you?
were you being honest when you said
you'd be there when i was ready?

do you still keep my number saved, love?
because it took me months
until i finally deleted yours
do you ever look up my profile
just to see what i've been up to?
does your dad ever ask how i've been doing?
do you look at the love island
episodes on the DVR,
one finger hesitating over the delete button,
wondering if i'll ever come back to you?

-    *i never even wanted to watch that show,*
     i just wanted to watch it with you

i think about leaning into you
about how natural it felt
how often you asked me to come closer
or how you always saved me a seat
i think of you, warm and loving and home
and it rips open a part of my heart
i thought i had stitched up forever

and i hate it, but i can't help but wonder:
do you try to remember what i felt like?
and do you ever think about
my head on your shoulder,
the wisps of my hair tickling your jaw
do you think about my feet up on your lap
or my head leaning back on your chest

do you remember the blankets
that you would wrap around us
on the old scratchy sofa in my backyard
or mosquito bites under the stars
or morning sunlight in your eyes
do you wish for sticky marshmallows
and swirling campfire smoke

tell me you think about it, love
tell me you dream about me
and wake up wondering
why i haunt you like a ghost
tell me you tell your new friends
that you'll stop talking about me but
my name remains on your lips like a curse

tell me that you miss the rasp
that would sneak into my voice after 2 am
tell me you can still hear
the melody of my sighs
that you miss my lyrical laugh
tell me you yearn for us
that you miss our friendship

tell me you think me about me, darling
tell me you've spent months aching
and trying to remember how i felt
tell me you can't breathe because
the memories of us catch in your throat
tell me you'll never forget me
because i've tried and i can't forget you

-    *tell me i'm unforgettable*

i let the tea get cold
because it is a monday morning,
the slow kind,
where i let the sunlight wash over me

and i take each step
with a sense of gratitude
where i open the windows
and listen to the birds

i remember another morning, long ago,
where you sat on the side of the couch
that i'm sitting on, and i made you tea
and smiled as i took in the sunlight

we hadn't slept that night
and i was exhausted
but i wanted to remember
everything about you

and looking back,
a part of me knew it wasn't going to last
and looking back,
i realize i want to start looking forward

so i let the tea get cold this morning
it is too strong
and smells too much
like late june and nostalgia

i let it get cold
and wrap myself in a blanket
after all, i can always
make another cup

-	*i stopped missing you today*

i've been writing love letters to you
but i think my love got lost in the mail
i sent you flowers only for you
to throw them in the trash
i dug them out to replant them
but they grew back dead

you tell me you love me just to fill the silence
the quiet a testament to the
chasm growing between us
when you're angry, your words cut deep
but poetry spills out of me,
staining your hands red as blood

i write you letters -
of love, of reconciliation, of peace
i immortalize you in ink and
fall in love with the pages
you rip them up in front of my eyes
as you tell me i'm so talented
as you throw them in flames to fuel your fury

i've been writing love letters
for as long as i can remember
it never mattered who i was addressing them to
i hold on to love that has left me long ago
even as my letters return back to their sender

all my life, i've been sending love letters
like they have no worth
to recipients who never deserved it
all my life, i've wanted someone
to write me love letters
but from now on, i'll be writing them to myself

-    *love letters to myself*

acknowledgements

if i could write love letters to everyone who
made this possible, they would go something
like this...

to mumma and daddy: thank you for not just
believing in my dreams but actively helping me
achieve them. to summer: thank you for being
my biggest cheerleader and my favourite sister.

to my wonderful grandparents and my extended
family: thank you for your prayers and your
constant support.

to my friends: thank you for being my platonic
soulmates and for reading these poems over and
over again until you knew them by heart, i
couldn't have done this without you.

to all of my english teachers and writing mentors
over the years: thank you for your feedback and
advice, no matter how harsh or how kind, for all
of it has made me better.

last but not least, to aunty nish: thank you for
inspiring my love of writing and for being my
guiding force throughout life - i'll miss you
forever and i love you present tense.

www.ingramcontent.com/pod-product-compliance
Lightning Source LLC
LaVergne TN
LVHW010925200726
843509LV00013B/2073